THE JOURNEY TO INNERPEACE

Rev. Paul A. Feider

AVE MARIA PRESS
Notre Dame, Indiana 46556

Cover design: Katherine A. Robinson
Printed and bound in the United States of America.

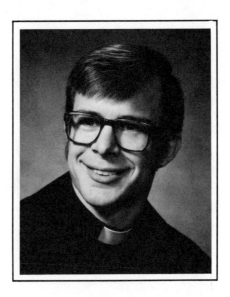

Rev. Paul Feider is an associate pastor of St. Peter's
Catholic Community in Oshkosh, Wisconsin, where he is
also active in leading scripture study programs and Life in
the Spirit Seminars. He is also a member of the Association of Christian Therapists. Father Feider did
undergraduate studies in Austria and holds a Master's of
Divinity degree from the St. Francis School of Pastoral
Ministry. He is the author of *The Christian Search for Meaning in Suffering* and *Paul's Letters for Today's Christians* (both
from Twenty-Third Publications).

CONTENTS

Foreword
by Barbara Shlemon, R.N.

It was in Malvern, Pennsylvania, at a national conference for the Association of Christian Therapists (A.C.T.) that I first met Father Paul Feider. A Milwaukee physician, Dr. Bernard Klamecki, had invited him to attend the five-day gathering of health care professionals and pastoral care ministers.

Although our conversation at that time was very brief, I remember being impressed with Father Paul's tranquillity of spirit and his quiet determination to learn. He sincerely wanted to understand the ministry of healing prayer in order to incorporate this gift of the Holy Spirit into his priesthood and he appeared willing to do whatever necessary to accomplish this goal. Apparently he found A.C.T. a helpful vehicle to foster spiritual growth because he continued to attend subsequent conferences providing opportunities to discuss our common interests in the healing ministry. These sharings enabled me to see a depth of wisdom beyond his years in this

young priest, and to appreciate Father Paul's
ability to communicate complex scriptural truths
in a simple uncomplicated language.

The Journey to Inner Peace reflects these at-
tributes as Father Paul describes the journey
within ourselves to attain the treasure Jesus
promised to his followers,

> " 'Peace' is my farewell to you,
> my peace is my gift to you."

Repeatedly after his resurrection Jesus appeared
to his disciples using the greeting, "Peace be with
you," thus reminding us of the importance at-
tached to this virtue. Throughout the gospels
Jesus taught the way of life which will bring harmonious blend to body, mind and spirit.

Modern medicine now recognizes the need
for peace when physicians refuse to perform
surgery on persons exhibiting high tension which
could precipitate complications. They know the
fear response of the mind will definitely affect the
body's ability to move toward wholeness. Most
physicians also believe the majority of patients
seen in their offices are suffering from
psychosomatic illnesses: physical problems created
by a lack of inner peace. As the world becomes
more and more infused with the fear of nuclear
annihilation, our society is demonstrating a growing propensity toward the stress-related illnesses.

Father Paul's book encourages the reader to
admit the fears which create barriers to tranquillity, asking Jesus to show us his way of deal-
ing with conflict, anger, doubt and confusion.

The author freely shares his own life experiences of learning to walk in the "mystery of the silent confidences of Jesus" citing ways we can better utilize the avenues to grace available to us. His explanation of the sacrament of reconciliation and its relationship to healing brings fresh insights to this valuable gift of God's forgiving love. Father Paul finds it ironic that the sacrament which formerly instilled so much fear in the hearts of many Catholics now emerges as a place for healing.

During my own years of involvement with the health care profession, I have heard numerous counselors lament that their most difficult task was helping persons get rid of the bondage of personal guilt when they had no belief in the atonement of Jesus Christ. This constant sense of condemnation completely prevents valid thinking or rational judgment, hence the problem of escapism in our society. If there is no freedom from sin, then true peace is impossible.

Father Paul's book examines the process of unbinding the painful hurts in our lives through the exercise of inner healing prayer. Recently published literature from the scientific community is confirming the profound effects of early childhood memories on the human psyche. The conscious mind may have long forgotten the pain of rejection or separation but the imprint remains on the unconscious mind creating various degrees of internal turmoil.

Using examples from his ministry, Father

Paul illustrates the release from emotional bondage by inviting Jesus Christ to transform past experiences from darkness into light. Inner peace
becomes a reality through the cleansing action of
the Savior who "bore our suffering and endured
our sorrows." There is a great emphasis on the
need for peace in our troubled world as large
numbers of concerned persons are daily joining
the ranks of nonviolence to seek an end to the
insanity of nuclear weaponry. But the movement
toward peace can never be fully accomplished until true inner peace reigns in our hearts through
repentance, conversion and healing. May the
message contained in this book bring inner peace
to all who are willing to apply these principles to
their lives.

INTRODUCTION

*Though he was harshly treated, he submitted
and opened not his mouth.*

(Isaiah 53:7)

For many years I have been awed by the
silence of Jesus as he was unjustly condemned to
death. Perhaps it has such an effect on me
because I feel within myself at times the desire to
retaliate in the face of injustice. Something in me
is unresolved and wishes to burst to the surface
and be expressed. Perhaps Jesus' silence intrigues
all of us because our inner fears would push us to
be defensive; our insecurities would tempt us to
be less than honest. Perhaps it captures us
because we live in a world arming itself out of
fear and then fearing its own defenses. The
mysterious silence of a man being condemned to
death is unnerving! What is he made of? What
has happened inside him that he does not need
to fight back? What has he done to face this
treacherous situation with such courage? What
does his silence say to me?

13

As I seek to give spiritual guidance to people, I see the pain of misunderstandings and the unresolved violence in relationships. I see the bondage of fear that imprisons the hearts of broken people searching for wholeness. I cringe at the reactions of people when the strength of will can no longer hold in the reservoir of repressed feelings. I ask myself, how can they be led to the God-man whose life journey I read in the gospel? Can his silent witness make a difference? Is the love he showed in the face of injustice and violence still able to bring peace?

I read about this Silent Lover and imagine the people who met him, who talked with him, who dared to follow his path, people like you and me. They walked with the Master, listened to his words, watched his gestures, and their lives were radically transformed. What power this relationship had! I marvel at the awesome silence of a man whose love empowered his disciples to stand in quiet self-assurance as the leaders of the land debated the destiny of their lives. From frightened fishermen they journeyed to become courageous witnesses. From where did they draw such great confidence? Where did all their fears go? How did they face impending suffering and even death with such boldness?

Perhaps we can begin to unravel the mystery of their bold silence by journeying within ourselves. What is it that makes us insecure in the face of certain situations? What undermines our convictions and our dreams? What are the roots of our fears? Perhaps from little on we have never felt affirmed or accepted for who we are. Perhaps one of our sins has never been released by the loving mercy of God. Maybe we have never learned to talk with God, to hear his voice in our lives, and so we journey along, alone and afraid.

This book dares to journey into the mystery of the silent confidence of Jesus, and those who followed him. It is a journey into ourselves. It seeks to discover the walls that cause fear and the journey that makes courage possible. That journey toward inner peace may not be easy, yet it seems necessary to discover the real meaning of life. If life is worth living, it is worth living in peace!

CHAPTER 1

When Jesus saw their faith he said to the paralytic, "Have courage, son, your sins are forgiven."

(Matthew 9:2)

THE FEAR OF
NOT BEING LOVABLE

Why am I afraid to say what I really mean? Why do I feel so nervous inside all the time? Why am I so scared to die? Why am I so scared to live? These and other questions reveal that many people live in the bondage of inner fear. The roots of those fears can sink deep into our past lives touching various areas of our conscious and unconscious existence. The errors we make seem to be a primary source of fear and insecurity. We fear that we are no longer lovable by anyone, including our Creator.

My years as a priest and minister of healing tell me that sin is a major source of insecurity. So often my journey with people to wholeness takes us back to unresolved sins and the consequent actions and reactions that still ripple through their lives. There seems to be something in us that gets frightened when we fail. This must have

been evident to the writer of the book of
Genesis. The first man and woman became fearful and hid when their relationship with the
Creator was marred by a selfish act. The peace
and security of the Creator's dream was unsettled. Fear entered the world, and only the
silent yes of the Creator's Son would be able to
restore real peace again.

As I listen to human hearts in the sacrament
of reconciliation, I am convinced that unrepented
sin is a very significant factor at the root of many
people's fears. From the child who tells me that
he stole three candy bars and is scared what will
happen if anyone finds out, to the adolescent
who slept with her boyfriend and is afraid of being rejected, to the husband who swindled some
money and fears for the fate of himself and his
family, the stories reveal that sin makes us fearful. It shakes loose the inner confidence that was
created in us by God.

Sin makes us feel unworthy, and often
unlovable and scared. We see this in Peter as he
recognized the Lord after his miraculous catch of
fish. He felt unworthy because of his past sins.
He felt uncomfortable in the presence of the one
who could set him free, and so he cried out,
"Leave me, Lord. I am a sinful man" (Lk 5:8).
How often have we felt that fear of unworthiness? Do we ever try to hide those moments of
weakness from the one who is so strong, so good?
Yet the pain of hiding only intensifies the fear.
Jesus who could bring us peace is shut out at the

time when we most need him. Time only magnifies the feeling of unworthiness and fear, and makes the door to freedom less and less accessible.

Perhaps we feel at times like Simon the Pharisee (Lk 7:36-50), wining and dining Jesus in the chamber of our heart, hoping he will not ask embarrassing or discomforting questions, and yet secretly wishing that someone would set us free. We find security in pointing a finger at someone else, just as Simon points his at the intruding "public sinner." The Master's abundant mercy leaves us wishing we could tell it like it is. The woman's openness and deep love is Simon's envy, and like him we cover our pain with ridicule and misjudgments. As in the story, our peers question his power to forgive, but we know that we would give anything to hear those freeing words for ourselves. "Your faith has been your salvation. Now go in peace" (Lk 7:50). We long for that peace but remain entrenched in unworthiness and fear.

Sin can unsettle us and drain away our courage. The discord of broken relationships echoes within our being and with time leaves us unsure of our true identity. We can become afraid of who we are and in frustrated denial project our sinfulness on convenient victims. The story of the woman caught in adultery (Jn 8:1-11) is an example of such projection. I read that story and marvel at how true to life it is. I discover in my life the temptation to "throw stones" at someone else rather than deal with my own sinfulness. I hear people verbally stoning their neighbors or fellow citizens, and I wonder what sins they are covering up. I watch marriage partners stone each other for their imperfections, and I question whether they even know where the sin began. Jesus' words, "Let the man among you who has no sin be the first to cast a stone at her," can snap us loose from such defensive projection and begin the process of personal reconciliation.

If, indeed, sin lies at the base of our fears, then our decision for repentance or the forgiveness of one who has sinned against us is the beginning of new courage and security. That decision is the most freeing decision that some people make in their lifetime. Choosing to resolve errors of the past brings unexpected new peace to many. At a time in history when some fear the extinction of the sacrament of reconciliation, I find more and more people discovering the freeing power of its words and gestures. How ironic that the sacrament that perhaps in the past instilled so much fear in Catholics and non-Catholics alike, now emerges as a place of inner healing and security. What may have felt like a place of judgment for a time in history is being rediscovered as a place of peace. We all need to know and feel that our mistakes do not eternally bind us. What a privilege to hear someone minister the personal redeeming love of Jesus upon our failures.

My years of ministering the sacrament of reconciliation have taught me much about the freeing and healing effects of hearing forgiveness spoken to the sinner. I continue to be mystified at the freeing power of Jesus' words, "Courage, son, your sins are forgiven" (Mt 9:2). As I try to reenact Jesus' encounter with my voice, my hands and my embrace, I watch loads of pain and fear being lifted from the hearts of his people. I stand in awe at the power of these forgiving moments. I hear the children say, "It made me feel so peaceful inside. It felt like a big load was lifted off of me." I rejoice with teenagers and adults as we share the closing embrace of this sacrament. In perplexed amazement they tell me, "I feel like a brand-new person. The fear is gone! It feels so good."

I stand in awesome recognition that their freeing encounter has been with the Lord. Their comments remind me of perhaps the most powerful portrayal of the freeing mercy of Jesus captured in the pages of scripture—the story of the woman at the well (Jn 4:4-42).

Put yourself at the well around noon on this very ordinary day, and watch the gentle words of the tired God-man put someone at peace. Let his words, his eyes, his love minister to you.

The sun is hot and the would-be stranger makes a request seemingly for himself, only to free the woman who thirsts. "Give me a drink," he says, not because he is thirsty, but because the years of fear and the consequent defenses of the women need to be slowly disassembled.

"You are not supposed to talk to me," she retorts, hiding behind the defenses of cultural expectations. Like the man who "isn't supposed to cry" or the woman who "isn't supposed to object," she thinks that she has found a refuge for her fears. Jesus sees the fear inside of her and gently proceeds to focus on her thirst for freedom.

"I will give you living water," he says. Still holding out, the woman attempts to point out the impossibility of his offer.

"The well is deep," she says. Like us, she longs for peace, but is slow to allow in the real peacemaker. Finally, she asks for the stranger's gift, even though she does not fully understand.

"Go call your husband," he asks bluntly, for honesty is the price of his enticing offer. She makes one last attempt to cover her pain with an ironic statement about the men in her life.

"I have no husband," she replies, and her unspoken longing for someone to love her and free her to feel lovable is revealed in the silence of her saddened face. Jesus does not reprimand the verbal lie, but in a profound moment of healing affirmation recognizes her fear and compliments the unknown truth of her statement.

"You are right in saying you have no husband!" he says, and he begins to quench her hidden thirst. His love and acceptance set her free to reveal the dark spot in her life. The fear of unrepented sin is released and the thirst for a true lover is satisfied. The pains of her loneliness and the insecurity of her sin find a heart that understands.

The woman, now freed, is no longer concerned about her water jar, because she is no longer thirsty. She leaves her jar, goes back into town, and announces to the people that she met a man at the well who loved her and told her she was lovable.

Pause for a moment, and think about this situation. This woman who is known to move from man to man quite freely comes walking into town and says, "I met a man at the well!" What would be your response? "Another one! What's new in Shechem? Our loose woman met her seventh man!" This scene could conceivably have been spiced with ridiculing laughter. What is it then that makes her story at all credible? Why do the people respond the way they do? The stranger may have told her some things about her past, but her reconciled heart must have portrayed an obvious new peace, for "many people" stop what they are doing to come and see this man. Her presence has convinced them that he is not just "another man."

There were more thirsty people in that town, and the peace of one woman's freed heart brings them to the well. The decision of one woman to let down her defenses and confess her sin becomes a fountain within her proclaiming the love that never runs out.

This story is a story of you and me. The encounters we have with Jesus can make all the difference. Past serious sins or present failings can bind us in fear, but the love of Jesus is stronger than fear. Perhaps we cannot avoid sin, but we can avoid becoming imprisoned in it. Our humble, honest admission of failure followed by sorrowful repentance breaks the hold sin can have on us. Like the woman at the well, we can be set free in the warm embrace of the Master's mercy. The decision to accept his forgiveness makes us new people. The decision to forgive those who have sinned against us affords us new courage and freedom to live in peace. Setting others free makes us free, free to proclaim the life-giving love of Jesus with boldness.

At times, the freeing forgiveness of Jesus empowers us to forgive ourselves and to feel the forgiveness of others. This truth has been evident with people who are freed from the guilt of having an abortion. A woman recently came to me not sure why she always felt guilty and unworthy. One conversation brought out that seven years ago she had had an abortion. She said that she had confessed it, but somehow something felt unresolved inside. She had taken the first step of freedom, and now she was wondering how to take the next one. I told her that in the prayerful security of God's love she could imagine the aborted child at the age it would now be, determine its sex, give it a name, and see it resting in the arms of Jesus. Then she should hear the child forgive her for what she did, and be peaceful that it rests in the love of the Lord.

The woman was not ready to pray in this manner that day, but that night, in the quiet of her private prayer, she did. The next morning she called me in joy to tell me about the vision she had had of her aborted child. "It was a girl," she said, "and her name is Melissa! She forgave me for acting out of fear and misunderstanding seven years ago. I feel so peaceful to know that she is happy and that I will see her again. Thank you."

Such incidents make me very aware of the power of experiencing forgiveness. We must not only know it, but we must *experience* it. We must seek out people who will radiate the gentle mercy of Jesus to us, and then encourage us to set others free with the mercy that we have received. We may need someone who can help us hear the forgiveness of one who is no longer present to us. Like the people in the gospel stories, we must choose to let the mercy of Jesus set us free to be peaceful, free to feel lovable, because we have been created lovable by God.

PRAYER FOR RECONCILIATION

Lord, your care for me is overwhelming. Even when I turn away from you or ignore you, you remain quietly present, waiting for me to accept your freeing mercy. You desire so much to make me feel lovable, as you have created me. You see the prison of fear and sin that I put myself in, and you gently invite me to come out and live freely with you. Lord, give me the courage to receive your love for me. Help me to honestly admit and repent of all my past failings, in order that your mercy may free me of any bondage of fear caused by sin. Let me feel the deep peace of reconciliation. Give me the strength to forgive myself, that I may feel lovable and acceptable in your sight. Thank you, Lord, that this process has already begun. Thank you for being so patient and gentle with me. Amen.

GOD'S WORDS OF PEACE FOR REFLECTION

A clean heart create for me, O God,
    and a steadfast spirit renew within me.
Cast me not out from your presence,
    and your holy spirit take not from me
Give me back the joy of your salvation,
    and a willing spirit sustain in me.

(Psalm 51:12-14)

But now, thus says the LORD,
    who created you, O Jacob, and formed
        you, O Israel:
Fear not, for I have redeemed you;
    I have called you by name: you are mine.
When you pass through the water, I will be
        with you;
    in the rivers you shall not drown.
When you walk through fire, you shall not
        be burned;
    the flames shall not consume you.
For I am the LORD, your God,
    the Holy One of Israel, your savior.
I give Egypt as your ransom,
    Ethiopia and Seba in return for you.
Because you are precious in my eyes
    and glorious, and because I love you.

(Isaiah 43:1-4)

I will sprinkle clean water upon you to cleanse you from all your impurities, and from all your idols I will cleanse you. I will give you a new heart and place a new spirit within you, taking from your bodies your stony hearts and giving you natural hearts. I will put my spirit within you and make you live by my statutes, careful to observe my decrees. You shall live in the land I gave your fathers; you shall be my people, and I will be your God.

(Ezekiel 36:25-28)

Jesus said to them, "Who among you, if he has a hundred sheep and loses one of them, does not leave the ninety-nine in the wasteland and follow the lost one until he finds it? And when he finds it, he puts it on his shoulders in jubilation. . . . I tell you there will likewise be more joy in heaven over one repentant sinner than over ninety-nine righteous people who have no need to repent."

(Luke 15:4-5,7)

Other appropriate readings:

Psalm 32:1, 7
Psalm 100
Jeremiah 31:3
Matthew 9:2
Luke 5:30-32
John 4:10, 13-14

John 8:10-11
John 15:9, 15-16
Romans 5:6, 8
Ephesians 2:4
1 Timothy 1:15-16

CHAPTER 2

*Jesus said to him, "Today salvation has come
to this house. . . . The Son of Man has come to
search out and save what was lost."*

(Luke 19:9-10)

MEMORIES THAT BIND US

The recognition of our sin and the decision to receive forgiveness are the first steps toward inner security. The fear stemming from sin can often be quickly alleviated through the experience of God's overwhelming mercy. Sometimes, however, sin is only a symptom of some deeper pains. Our journey toward inner peace leads us to examine the memories that bind us in fear.

Fears can begin early in life. Willfully or unwillfully they are born in the silence of forgotten moments. I listen to the stories of people who were carried in the womb unwanted, or were brought into life unwelcomed, and I realize that they have not forgotten. Their feelings keep telling them that "something isn't right." I can hear between the lines that the forgiving waters of baptism did not wash away all the memories that bind them with insecurity.

31

I watch children living between mother and father, grandmother and babysitter, and I wonder if they will ever feel as though they belong to anyone. They look so small; yet I know their memory is collecting the fear of all these movements. People are providing for their "needs" but no one is affirming their hearts. They become adults with time, but time alone does not heal the memories or calm the inner fears. Many times it only makes the situation more intensely painful. Like the children in the gospel, they long for the secure touch of the Master's hand, and hope that it happens before they are scared away by those who do not understand (Mk 10:13-16).

As children, we all needed affirming accep-tance from someone who we knew truly cared. The lack of such love may have left pockets of insecurity in all of us, insecurity that for some has not yet been overcome.

Maybe our fearful memories were collected a little later in life. I am amazed, for example, as I watch little children in the classrooms I visit. I ask them questions about Jesus and I am struck by the hesitancy with which some of them dare to answer. I know that they have the knowledge in their heads, but the fear in their heart keeps it hidden within. The possibility of ridicule from onlooking peers keeps their knowledge in bon-dage. They would love to express what is inside them, but the sound of insensitive laughter would be too much to bear.

I see myself in those children. Perhaps you see yourself. Years of would-be attackers have kept us from being our fullest selves, and maybe even have caused us to retaliate at people who have entered our life later on. Our bodies have grown, and our minds have pushed those memories into unconsciousness, but the fear that was caused way back then still holds us captive.

Maybe such bondage is not so different from what held the "little man" in the gospel from living his life in peace. I speak of Zacchaeus (Lk 19:1-10). He is the man who desires to see Jesus, yet is unacceptable among his peers. The story tells us of a powerful encounter that sets the little man free.

Jesus is coming to town and this fearful little man wishes to meet him. The branches of a nearby tree give him the security he needs to get a view of the man who is passing through town. His captivity of fear and perhaps guilt is brought to an end by the inviting voice of the acclaimed traveler. "Zacchaeus, hurry down. I mean to stay at your house today." It was an invitation to let go of old securities. The assurance of love, the promise of fellowship, melts the memories of rejection and the little man begins a new life in freedom. The jeers of the one-time-fearful crowd are silenced by the confident words of the one-time-fearful man. The love and acceptance that freed him from his old securities give him space to repent of his retaliation. He now gives back all that he had taken in anger and resentment. He is now free to live again.

Is not that little man in all of us? Are we up
a tree at times in desperation because of what
others have done to us in our past? Do we live
with the memories of how we have been made to
feel little and unacceptable? Is that perhaps the
reason why we often retaliate in sinful ways? Like
the little man, we try to get even. When we get
in the right position, we "defraud" the innocent
person in payment for the unhealed damage that
someone else did to us. Perhaps we even take it
out on the people we love because they just happen to be there or because we are confident that
they will not fight back. At times we may "sur-
vive" off the poor people, the little ones who are
not able to retaliate, yet we feel up a tree in our
bondage.

The invitation to "come down" comes from
Jesus, and we know he wants to set us free. He
knows our bondage. He knows that the sins of
others and our own sin hold our memory and
our whole being in the grip of fear. He has come
to set us free, to stop the chain reaction of sin
that shakes one generation after another. He has
come to heal our memories that collect hurts
before they are inflicted unjustly upon another
"crowd of people." The power of his invitation
and the silence of his love make us aware that
our fearful memories have found an avenue for
freedom.

Leading people out of their bondage of fearful memories is often more complex and takes
longer than the process of freedom through

reconciliation. Memories establish patterns, and sometimes the security of the "tree" is more appealing than the freedom of wholeness found in the encounter of love. At some point a person must choose to journey out of old securities and to begin living in new patterns. It is the power of Jesus' unconditional love that makes these choices possible. Prayer support and affirmation from a caring community is often necessary to empower a fearful person to make these crucial choices. The challenge of a minister of healing is to radiate the love and acceptance of Jesus in such a profound way that the person cannot help but feel it. Since all of our personalities are different, I often work with a team of helpers, hoping that the individual in need will find healing security in one of us.

Once the person has felt the love of Jesus through at least one, we can begin the prayerful journey of inner healing. Through the gift of imagination, we slowly see Jesus walk back into the binding memories, letting our discerning hearts guide us. Together we imagine his words of acceptance and mercy. We envision the moments when harm had been done and see Jesus standing in those situations. Words that he spoke long ago to so many are now experienced as spoken to the fearful, hurting person. The love in those words brings new peace and security. All of this is done in a quiet environment of love and prayer.

Often this process of unbinding the grip of memories requires some education, for people do

not always know exactly what it is that causes
their reactions. Sometimes it is precisely this
unknown that causes them to be fearful. Any of
us may sense this fear at times. For example, do
you ever find yourself flying off the handle at
some innocent inquirer? Do you ever get enraged
to such an extent that you fear your own anger?
Do your reactions to little mistakes seem inap-
propriately severe? If this happens, we may sense
that something is not right, but we may not be
able to detect the source or sources of our anger.

I ask people in this situation to slowly walk
back through their past with Jesus alongside
them. As they take this quiet journey, they often
discover incidents from long ago where anger was
repressed into their unconscious. When we make
such a discovery, we stop and pray for healing,
asking forgiveness, or forgiving someone if
necessary. A journey like this can be frightening
and sometimes painful, but the security of one
who cares makes it possible. The new peace the
hurting person discovers makes it worthwhile.

At times the same inner journeys are taken
to uncover painful hurts of the past. The lack of
love and affirmation in childhood, whether
willfully or unwillfully caused, is often a source of
nagging pain and insecurity. Without blaming
anyone, we journey back into those memories
and let the love of Jesus fill those places in our
heart where we have not felt loved in a complete
way. Sometimes, too, it is necessary to ask Jesus
to cleanse us of the resentment and bitterness
that may have resulted from earlier moments of
not feeling loved.

Perhaps the greatest source of inner fear is childhood memories of insecurity. We have all had experiences of insecurity as children, but if these were not calmed by accepting love through our growing years, they may still have influence over us. They may remain as dark pockets of seemingly forgotten moments. It is sometimes hard to uncover them since the thought of approaching these dark areas makes an already frightened person even more fearful. I have found the image of the father wrapping his arms around the prodigal son (Lk 15:20) to be very powerful in calming these fears. This is particularly true for those who feel insecure about their sexuality. Experiencing themselves in the healing embrace of God often allows people to approach fearful hidden memories. Bathing the person in this secure love as they tell those fearful stories brings new peace to their whole being.

Whether we are seeking to release people from the memories of anger, hurt, or fear, the process is similar, namely, bathing them in the secure love of Jesus. Before all the patterns stemming from these memories disappear, the person may need to be soaked in this love many times. Once the initial journey is made, the accepting love of other caring people continues the healing process.

Often people are surprised at the power that unresolved memories can have over them, even after many years. I recall a woman who came to me because she felt unusually anxious in certain situations. "I can't understand why I react that way," she said. "I have all the securities I need, and yet I feel so insecure. I feel like I'm crazy sometimes." Our conversation led her to reveal that her mother had attempted to abort her. "But that was so many years ago," she explained. "I thought I was over it." Her experience was telling her that she was not "over" it.

As our conversation went on, I explained to her the powerful hold that past memories can have on a person. I pointed out that she was probably still in the grip of those memories of not being wanted and the fear of being destroyed. She expressed a sigh of relief to know that she was not "crazy" and that someone understood. I then shared with her the freeing and healing power of inviting Jesus into the painful experience. Once she understood the process, she asked if I would pray with her. Together we prayed, inviting Jesus in our words and imagination into that moment when the attempt was made on her life. We imagined Jesus loving her and holding her with a love that was not coming from her mother. Gradually, the woman felt a new peace come over her. She knew from that moment on that the source of her anxiety was gone. She left my office ready to let the Lord transform those feelings of insecurity created by this incident into feelings of peace.

Our memory is a beautiful gift, but sometimes it holds messages for years that even the power of repression cannot cover up.

Wishing the messages would go away only frustrates the situation. Our present situation may be secure and comfortable, but an unresolved memory can leave us fearful and insecure. As we have seen, the journey inward with Jesus consciously at our side can bring healing and new security to our lives. The same Jesus who walked the earth long ago can walk through the years of our lives and set us free.

As healing happens, we will see a change in our relationships and our responses to situations. Like Zacchaeus, we will see ourselves in a different way and gradually people will see and relate to us differently. We may have had a reputation for being touchy because anger poured through our words for years or often showed itself in very unexpected ways. We may have avoided certain gatherings because we feared the tears within that might embarrass us. We may have accumulated the security of possessions to hide the underlying insecurity that we feel. These relationships and patterns may or may not change quickly, but if we continue to bathe our memories in the conscious love of Jesus, they *will* change. No memory or its consequent fears can withstand the healing and freeing love of God poured out in Jesus the Lord.

PRAYER FOR THE
HEALING OF MEMORIES

Lord, you are so gentle and comforting. You have created me to be whole and at peace, yet you know that sinful situations have damaged that wholeness. I pray now that I might hear and accept your invitation to come down from my "tree" of false security, as Zacchaeus did, to discover the lasting security that you wish to give. Heal me, Lord, of any past anger, fear, or hurt that still binds my being. Walk through my whole life and let me feel your loving presence. Release from my memory anything that keeps me from living in true peace. Help me to truly forgive from my heart any person or persons who were part of creating those harmful memories. Thank you, Lord, that your healing love is always available to me, inviting me to wholeness and real inner peace. Lord, I accept your love right now as it pours into my heart. Thank you, Lord. Amen.

GOD'S WORDS OF PEACE FOR REFLECTION

You who dwell in the shelter of the Most
    High,
    who abide in the shadow of the
    Almighty,
Say to the LORD, "My refuge and my
    fortress,
    my God, in whom I trust."
For he will rescue you from the snare of the
    fowler,
    from the destroying pestilence.
With his pinions he will cover you,
    and under his wings you shall take refuge;
    his faithfulness is a buckler and a shield.
You shall not fear the terror of the night
    nor the arrow that flies by day;
Not the pestilence that roams in darkness
    nor the devastating plague at noon.
Though a thousand fall at your side,
    ten thousand at your right side,
    near you it shall not come.

(Psalm 91:1-7)

When Israel was a child I loved him,
    out of Egypt I called my son.
The more I called them,
    the farther they went from me,
Sacrificing to the Baals
    and burning incense to idols.
Yet it was I who taught Ephraim to walk,
    who took them in my arms;
I drew them with human cords,
    with bands of love;

I fostered them like one
   who raises an infant to his cheeks;
Yet, though I stooped to feed my child,
   they did not know that I was their healer.
                                   (Hosea 11:1-4)

Jesus said, "Come to me, all you who are weary and find life burdensome, and I will refresh you. Take my yoke upon your shoulders and learn from me, for I am gentle and humble of heart. Your souls will find rest, for my yoke is easy and my burden light."
                          (Matthew 11:28-30)

We have come to know and to believe
   in the love God has for us.
God is love,
and he who abides in love
abides in God,
and God in him. . . .
Love has no room for fear;
rather, perfect love casts out all fear.
                       (1 John 4:16,18)

Other appropriate readings:

Psalm 34:5-8	Luke 15:11-13, 17-20
Psalm 103:1-5	Luke 19:5-10
Psalm 116:1-6	John 17:9-11
Isaiah 35:4-6	James 5:13-15
Mark 1:40-42	1 John 3:1-2
Mark 5:33-34	

CHAPTER 3

Rising early the next morning, Jesus went off to a lonely place in the desert; there he was absorbed in prayer.

(Mark 1:35)

QUIETING
AND LISTENING

Reconciliation and inner healing can bring us peace and new security. This new peace, however, must be nurtured and sustained. One major reason, I find, why people do not have inner peace and security is that they have never learned how to hear and respond to the voice of the Lord, so they travel through life alone. Our life journey was never meant to be traveled alone. It can be very scary meeting life's challenges and making life's decisions without the calming assurance of the Creator's voice. This section of our journey leads us to discover ways to hear the gentle voice of God and feel the security it gives to our lives.

My own spiritual journey has taught me that real peace is only found by listening to the Master. I am one who would rather "do it my way," but experience has shown the fruits of "doing it his way." I do feel an inner peace in my life, but that peace is quickly unsettled and I become fearful when I stop listening and submitting to the Prince of Peace. Listening to the one who knows the ultimate purpose for our lives is our greatest source of peace.

In recent years I have come to feel in a very powerful way that Jesus' silent courage in the face of trials flowed from those quiet prayerful moments he spent with the Father. "Rising early the next morning, he went off to a lonely place in the desert; there he was absorbed in prayer" (Mk 1:35). He needed to renew himself in the affirming love of the Father to face the challenges of his mission. It is the bathing of himself in that love, I believe, that empowered him to respond to the sick with such compassion, and to his attackers with such inner strength and courage. Like Jesus, each one of us must quiet ourselves to absorb this inner peace.

Every spiritual journey is unique and special. My years in spiritual direction have shown me that the Lord speaks to each person in his own way. There are no hard and fast ways of learning Jesus' peace; there are only the footprints of those who live that peace.

The inner decision to *choose to listen* to his voice is the first crucial step toward inner peace. It means that we freely decide to act upon what we hear. This is a commitment to obedience, an obedience that was at the center of Jesus' life. "Son though he was, he learned obedience from what he suffered; and when perfected, he became a source of eternal salvation for all who obey him" (Heb 5:8-9). This initial decision to choose to submit to God's voice is often frightening at first. The insecurity of trying to make it on our own, however, when we think about it, is much more frightening. The knowledge of some guiding words for our lives cannot help but make us more secure and confident in our choices.

I will never forget the time in my life when a concerned spiritual director encouraged me to start listening to the Lord each day. In my proud style, I assured him that I had six and a half years of seminary training, and I did not need someone to tell me how to pray! That evening, in the quiet of my chapel visit, I had to swallow my words. I realized for the first time in my life that I had never really listened to the Lord. Rather, I had told him what I was doing and thanked him for being there to help. In that quiet moment of discovery, I felt overwhelmed with the realization that he loved me very dearly. It was as if I heard him say to me, "Paul, I appreciate all that you do, but do you know how much I love you? For years I have been watching you, waiting for you to slow down and feel my deep love for you."

It was after that encounter that I began to experience God's personal love for me and the security of that feeling. It was then that I also realized the love of God flowing through the pages of scripture. I began to recognize the many beautiful people he put into my life journey to express his personal love for me. I began to respond to situations differently knowing that every event somehow fit into his loving plan even if I did not understand it at the time. From that time on I have known an inner security in my life, a deep sense that the Creator was walking at my side.

Perhaps you have had a similar experience in life; perhaps you long for it. It can happen in various ways, but at some point there must be an inner decision to submit to the voice of Jesus. This decision becomes significant only to those who follow it with an ongoing process of surrendering every facet of their lives to the Lord's will. This process is gradual and gentle, for the Creator is always careful with his people. Isaiah captures this characteristic of God when he writes, "A bruised reed he shall not break, and a smoldering wick he shall not quench" (Is 42:3). Little by little the Lord prods us to let go of each area of our being, so that his peace can reign there. Our initial decision to listen to him is followed by a decision to continue the process.

People often ask me, "What can I do to continue this journey toward inner peace?" I can tell them what I have found to be significant and essential for me. It is the "going off alone" to be in communion with the Father. It involves a commitment to quieting ourselves on a consistent basis. At some point in our life, the desire for inner peace must become so strong that we make the commitment of time and effort to seek it and sustain it.

There are various patterns for quieting ourselves. Quentin Hakenwerth, S.M., in the book *In His Likeness*, speaks of five silences or ways of making our whole being attentive to the voice of God. He mentions the silence of our words, our nonverbal signs, our mind, our passions, and our imagination. Reflection upon these silences has helped me quiet myself and be more receptive to inner messages.

Considering the silence of words, for example, we realize how often we fill our environment with noise. The message of God necessary for our inner peace often gets squelched under less important words. The gift of peace which we all long for gets traded for less significant pleasures. I have discovered through the years the crucial need to have silence, to stop speaking, to turn off the radio, the television, and just take time to be quiet. We are surrounded by word, words, and more words. I wonder why.

I sense at times the temptation to hide in the false security of noise. We can get very used to noise, either from television and radios, or from our idle conversation. The pattern of such noise may keep us from journeying within and facing what we find there. Such hiding from ourselves only causes more fear. Quieting the noise in our world is necessary to dissolve such fear and move toward peace. This part of the journey entails discovering the moments in a day when we can simply be quiet with our God. The drive to and from work, the hours spent folding wash, the moments waiting for the bus, or the relaxing time at the end of a day can become precious listening moments.

Not only must we utilize these moments for quiet listening, but it is also necessary to take special moments in every day for quiet prayer when nothing else is going on. My half hour in the morning quietly sitting and pondering the words of scripture is the most strengthening time of my day. The quieting effect of time alone with the Lord is necessary for inner peace. The choice to make that time a primary value in my busy schedule is one of the best choices I have ever made.

Part of quieting ourselves also involves uncluttering our minds and hearts. They can be so filled with unnecessary data that it is almost impossible to take in the quieting voice of God. Silencing our minds and hearts means conscious-ly choosing which messages from books, magazines, movies, etc., we will allow to enter our being. Putting on the mind of Christ means being selective about what it is that we allow to consume us. Perhaps this is similar to what John meant when he wrote, "If anyone loves the world, the Father's love has no place in him" (1 Jn 2:15).

The process of quieting our minds and hearts begins with the realization that we do not *have to* read, or see, or listen to everything that comes our way. It involves examining our habits to see if we are selecting growthful material to enter our consciousness and emotions. That choice is our decision to a greater extent than we may realize. We can choose. If we wish to soak in the peace of Jesus, then we must choose to put out those things that distract us from him. Finding inner peace means creating space for that peace. God is constantly desiring to enter our consciousness, yet he stands at the mercy of our free decision to clear space and welcome him in. With his presence comes his inner peace.

As we grow in the quieting process, we may notice that certain feelings or passions distract us. They can be annoying. They each long for some of our time, like screaming children around a mother wishing to visit with her neighbor. Ignoring them does not make them go away. Like the wise mother we may need to introduce them to the friend and make them feel acceptable, affirmed and important. Acknowledging our feelings to our "Friend" in prayer is sometimes awkward, even though he already knows them. It does make our conversation with him much easier. We may even have to involve our feelings in the conversation for a while. At times this may need to be followed by the inner discipline of telling our passions to wait until this important visit is finished. This process of quieting our passions may be the most difficult, but the voice of God can begin to penetrate our being before we have this completely mastered.

Another facet of silencing our passions I have found helpful is becoming aware of our tendencies in life or the ways we have been taught to think and feel. To do this we might ask ourselves questions such as, What image of God have I grown up with? How securely was I loved through my childhood? What expressions of ideas or emotions were permissible in my family? These kinds of questions can help us get in touch with our life story and the people and events that influence the ways we relate to life. Being aware of these tendencies can help us distinguish the voice of God from our own inner voice. This part of the silencing process is often best done on a retreat or during an extended reflective period with the help of a spiritual director.

Once we create space through silencing ourselves, the word of God begins to fill the new quiet places in a very gentle yet powerful way. When I dare to listen and silence myself, the words of scripture I read every day become personal messages of God's love for me. These messages help me make more peaceful and patient responses to the people and events that enter my life. As I work with groups of people in what I call Spiritual Enrichment Seminars (six consecutive weekly meetings helping people grow in a deeper spiritual relationship with God), I notice the same pattern. They come back after a week of prayerful listening and share the excitement of how one or another scripture passage spoke to them that week in a totally new way. They notice a new peace and vision which changes their responses to people around them.

One man told me how his reflection on a few verses of scripture at noon for his "lunch break" changed the way he related to people the rest of the afternoon. He said, "They all felt like brothers and sisters to me after I listened to Jesus' words." A crucial part of growing in inner peace is giving the word of God space to transform our minds and hearts.

Bathing ourselves in the scriptures can help us to know God and the power of his love in our lives. This transforming power of God's word is described by a woman named Norma. She writes, "Ten months ago my life was in darkness, although I didn't know it to be exactly that. There were just so many things in my life that seemed wrong. I had feelings of guilt, depression, anger and anxiety. I just couldn't cope with things anymore. I was screaming and yelling at my children all the time and arguing with my husband. I knew I was miserable. I had to talk with someone who could be objective, compassionate and confidential, so I finally called my parish priest."

I remember Norma's visit. Her words told me that her search for relief was desperate, and her many tears told me that her pains were deep. Her heart needed to be soaked in love. I thought of places where she could be immersed in the love of God's word and his community. I suggested the Spiritual Enrichment Seminars to her. She decided to come. She writes, "I went only because I was desperate! I did not know what else to do. What I had tried failed, and if this could put my life in some kind of order and give me true happiness, then I was game!"

Though her motive may not have been perfect, she did come to the seminars, and the word of God together with community support showed its transforming power. She describes the process this way. "I read the daily scripture passage that was suggested as part of the seminars. It was as if the words spoke directly to me. It was as if God was gradually healing my pains. Each week we shared what the words of scripture were saying to us. Some of us were high, some of us were low. Some of us hurt so deeply inside that we could not share, so we just soaked everything in. It was the start of a new direction in my life."

After the six weeks of seminars, Norma continued to attend our weekly prayer gatherings. I could see that God was healing her and setting her free from the bondage of the past. Her guilt, depression, anger and anxiety are gone. She now is part of our healing ministry. She radiates a peace and a joy that is inspiring to me, since I know that she still experiences pain from her arthritis. She writes of herself, "Once there was darkness in my life, but now there is light—a whole new meaning to life itself. I'm not saying that life is not difficult at times, but now I have God's word to guide me through the storms in my life, and when it is peaceful and happy, I again have God's words to praise him for his great glory. Reading the bible has become a part of my daily living. It helps me to be prepared for my day, whatever it might be. After being on this good earth almost 40 years, I feel that a seed has just been planted in me. I am finally growing into the person and the disciple that God has intended me to be."

Immersing ourselves in the word of God can happen in a number of ways. As I mentioned earlier, the most powerful time for me is alone in the quiet of my room. I dwell on the poetic verses of the psalms, and then randomly open to the life-giving words of the New Testament. Reflection on the readings during Mass is also a calming experience, although often I am distracted by the homily that I plan to give. My own study of scripture in preparation for teaching has at times left me pondering a brand-new insight. I have felt a peace and security grow out of learning the ways of Jesus from the gospels and seeing his strength in his disciples.

Besides these private ways of listening for God's voice, I have come to know a way of communal listening. Weekly I gather with people from the area who are each seeking to listen to the Lord. In the quiet of the Lord's presence, we read the scripture passage that has spoken to us personally during the week. This reading is often followed by a short personal prayer. Through the course of the evening there slowly emerges a common theme from these readings. This ongoing process of immersing ourselves in the word of

God has had a powerful healing and calming effect on us. We can be helpful to each other in hearing the voice of our common Lord.

I believe that within our Catholic heritage we are discovering a whole new source of power in the word of God. The new emphasis on scripture as part of the sacraments has made those events a more powerful opportunity to experience the Lord's presence. I see God's word bringing peace and healing to people in the sacraments of reconciliation and anointing. I hear people tell me of the inner strength they receive from the word of God during liturgies when they have been quietly attentive to the power in that word.

If this process of quieting ourselves and hearing the voice of God seems to go slowly, take heart and be patient with yourself, for you are in good company! It cannot help but comfort us to notice how the apostles, even after being with the Master himself, misunderstood his words and completely missed his message at times. When Jesus announced to the Twelve that he would have to suffer much and be put to death, they could not comprehend it. Their own emotions and their learned expectations made it impossible for them at that time to absorb that message (Mk 8:31-33). They were not yet used to hearing God's voice. Only very slowly would they learn to judge situations "by God's standards," and when they did, they became changed people. Their struggle to listen bore its fruit as they stood in silent courage in the face of persecution. The quiet voice of God within them made all the difference. Though our own process of silencing and listening may take time, gradually we will begin to feel the security of the Master's voice.

PRAYER FOR INNER QUIET

Lord, I want to be quiet inside and hear your words for me. I know that your voice can give true peace to my heart. Give me the strength to quiet myself each day that your voice may truly be the guide in my life. Fill me with the courage to trust and obey the messages you give to me. Let me feel through your words your deep love for me, that I may know the real peace you have promised. Thank you, Lord, for continually speaking words of love to me, even when I block them out with my noise. Be patient with me as I slowly create quiet spaces in my life for you. You are indeed good to me, and I love you. Amen.

GOD'S WORDS OF PEACE FOR REFLECTION

O Lord, you have probed me and you know
   me;
   you know when I sit and when I stand;
   you understand my thoughts from afar.
My journeys and my rest you scrutinize,
   with all my ways you are familiar.
Even before a word is on my tongue,
   behold, O LORD, you know the whole of
      it.
Behind me and before, you hem me in
   and rest your hand upon me.
Such knowledge is too wonderful for me;
   too lofty for me to attain.
Where can I go from your spirit?
   from your presence where can I flee?
If I go up to the heavens, you are there;
   if I sink to the nether world, you are
      present there.

                              (Psalm 139:1-8)

Sing out, O heavens, and rejoice, O earth,
   break forth into song, you mountains,
For the LORD comforts his people
   and shows mercy to his afflicted.
But Zion said, "The LORD has forsaken me;
   my Lord has forgotten me."
Can a mother forget her infant,
   be without tenderness for the child of her
      womb?
Even should she forget,
   I will never forget you.

See, upon the palms of my hands I have
    written your name.

(Isaiah 49:13-16)

"Do not let your hearts be troubled.
Have faith in God
and faith in me.
In my Father's house there are many
    dwelling places;
otherwise, how could I have told you
that I was going to prepare a place for you?
I am indeed going to prepare a place for
    you,
and then I shall come back to take you with
    me,
that where I am you also may be."

(John 14:1-3)

He comforts us in all our afflictions and thus
enables us to comfort those who are in trouble,
with the same consolation we have received from
him. As we have shared much in the suffering of
Christ, so through Christ do we share abundantly
in his consolation. If we are afflicted it is for your
encouragement and salvation, and when we are
consoled it is for your consolation, so that you may
endure patiently the same sufferings we endure.

(2 Corinthians 1:4-6)

Other appropriate readings:

Psalm 4:2, 9	Mark 10:13-16
Psalm 46:2-4	Luke 11:9, 13
Psalm 145:8-9, 18	John 6:35
Isaiah 55:1-3	1 Corinthians 10:13
Jeremiah 29:11-14	Revelation 3:20
Mark 1:35	

CHAPTER 4

*"Teach them to carry out everything I have
commanded you.
And know that I am with you always, until
the end of the world!"*

(Matthew 28:20)

THE SECURITY OF
THE MASTER'S VOICE

The words of Jesus heard in our hearts can make a big difference in how we respond to life situations. His voice gives hope where there is despair, peace where there is insecurity, courage where there is fear; it proclaims life in situations that seem like death. It was the words of Jesus together with his harmonious witness that changed the lives of people he met and instilled in them the conviction to change others. The power of his word spoken long ago waits to be unleashed in our hearts. The strength of his love that instilled courage in his disciples and brought healing to the people he met, still flows from his living presence among us. This section of the journey toward inner peace allows us to reflect on what we might expect to hear after we quiet the inner voices and listen to the Master.

One of the most profound and significant acts of Jesus, I believe, was his compassion for the sick. He was "moved with pity" or "filled with tenderness" at the sight of them, and he reached out in warmth and concern. Now perhaps his response does not at first seem revolutionary, but think of the context and the consequences of his compassionate gestures.

In Jesus' time, it was customary to treat sick people with contempt because their sickness was often thought to be a punishment for their sins, or their parents' sins (Ex 20:5; Dt 5:9). Jesus' response of compassion for sick people, then, was quite unique. It did not answer all questions about the origins of illness and the consequent suffering, but it clearly eliminated the notion that sickness is a punishment from God. If illness were a punishment from the Father, then Jesus' response of compassion and healing would have been contrary to the Father's plan. Such disunity was not possible in his nature since he was one with the Father. His action in regard to sickness clearly reveals God on the side of the sick person. In his love and compassion he stands *with* the sick person, desiring to eliminate the illness. His resurrection from the dead added to this revelation the deeper understanding that no illness is ultimate; not even death can withstand the power of God's love. Can you sense how revolutionary his actions were? Can you feel the security and courage that flowed from his unique response to the sick? Can you imagine the inner peace that he brought to those who were ill, and still brings to us today? He is on *our* side, not against us.

It amazes me at times that this good news can get lost so quickly. So often I meet with people who are ill, and one of their first remarks is, "I guess God is punishing me." How sad that they sense God against them in their illness when he has so powerfully revealed himself to be on their side in the illness. At a time when they so need to feel wrapped in the healing love of God, they abandon the central message of Jesus and find themselves in fear, loneliness and insecurity.

Perhaps you have found yourself or a friend in this situation. The message found in Jesus' word is that he is with you. That is the security of the Master's voice, his life example. His healing ministry together with his resurrection from the dead gives us the power to face illness and even death with courage, for both must bow to the eternal love he has for us.

This message also applies to the crisis situations we meet in life. Jesus came that we might have life and have it to the full (Jn 10:10). He does not punish us with illness or crisis. Things may happen to us because of our mistakes, or the mistakes of someone else, or the laws of nature, or for some other reason, but God is *with us* to deal with the situation. That is the revolutionary message of Jesus! Sometimes we punish ourselves. Sometimes others punish us, but God is always with us to find some ultimate peace and life in those situations. Jesus emptied himself completely and came among us to proclaim his desire to give us life. He stood in the midst of death and said, "I want you to have life." His living word keeps saying that to us. John writes, "God so loved the world that he gave his only Son, that whoever believes in him may not die but may have eternal life. God did not send the Son into the world to condemn the world, but that the world might be saved through him" (Jn 3:16-17). That word gives a new perspective to every life event. Jesus' words and his witness allow us to face life with courage, assuming we welcome him to walk with us on our journey.

The realization that Jesus is with us in times of crisis is truly a source of new life and courage. I have never felt his sustaining presence more strongly than at the time of my father's death. I had preached about resurrection, but now I felt the comfort of that message. The words I found in scripture at that time were, "I am the good shepherd, I know my sheep and my sheep know me" (Jn 10:14). I knew that Dad knew the Shepherd, and I felt peaceful that he was in good hands.

It was the peace of the Shepherd that gave me the courage and the strength to celebrate Dad's Mass of Resurrection. I knew the day I was ordained that this was probably the hardest thing I would ever have to do. My family wondered for a while if I would celebrate the funeral, since they knew the deep love that Dad and I shared. I knew that it would not be easy, and yet it was the Shepherd's voice that told me it was possible.

Trusting in his voice, I chose to celebrate and preach the Mass in honor of the man who taught me the Shepherd's name and his love. Yes, it was hard. I did not pretend that it was easy, but in the midst of the pain, I felt a powerful sustaining love that I had never known before. I knew that Jesus was with me. The love I felt that day has given me new courage to step out in faith and accept challenges that I know I cannot handle on my own.

Jesus' desire to be with his people in time of need showed itself also in his response to repentant sinners. He expressed his oneness with them by sitting at their table, not because he condoned sin, but because he wanted to be there to rescue the persons overcome by sin as soon as they indicated a desire to be free. This gesture continues to speak peace and new courage to anyone who has experienced the insecurity of sin. Jesus shows that no sin is beyond forgiveness. Only our refusal to accept forgiveness can keep us in sin's grasp and the fear that flows from it.

Jesus could find good in everyone, and if they received his love, they also received a sense of belonging. The personal risk at which he came among the sick and the sinners had to demonstrate very clearly that he truly cared. He risked his life to tell them that they were lovable, and he poured out his love to show them that they could be well. Jesus' words and actions toward the ill and those who had sinned gave them new hope and courage. Hearing those

words and experiencing those actions in our lives
can do the same for us. The voice of the Master
made incarnate in our lives gives us true peace.

If there is another strong peace-giving
message in the words and actions of Jesus, it is
the way he responded to the ridicule and false accusations that were dealt him. The crucifix sym-
bolizes this unique response. John writes, "Just as
Moses lifted up the serpent in the desert, so must
the Son of Man be lifted up, that all who believe
may have eternal life in him" (Jn 3:14-15). The
crucifix is a symbol of real love and inner peace.
Jesus lifted up on the cross represents all the pain
that he endured to proclaim forgiveness, healing
and new life to us. It represents the pain that
Jesus felt long before the nails were driven in, the
rejection of his relatives, the rejection and
ridicule of the leaders of his time, and the
betrayal of his disciples.

Jesus on the cross is a life-giving symbol
because there he demonstrates a response to rejection and ridicule that is unique and powerful
for all time. Jesus never retaliates. He never
returns anger for anger, or injustice for injustice.
He speaks out against unjust and false situations,
and then his silence becomes a proclamation of
faith that the ultimate truth will defend itself. His
silence is not a submission to injustice, but a submission to the Father's will. It is the silence of
having "commended his spirit into the hands of
the Father" (Lk 23:46). His awesome silence at
his trial says that the truth had been spoken, and

those who could not receive it would condemn themselves to death. His silence speaks of true peace. The cross and the resurrection show us the power of that peace.

It seems that Jesus could stand in silence because he did not stand alone; he was in full union with his Father, a union of perfect love. It seems he could stand in silence because he never became imprisoned in his suffering. He never allowed his wounds to become infected with the poison of revenge or self-pity. Suffering that could have caused him to become self-centered, even less human, did not. Wounds that could have destroyed him, did not. Only when wounds become poisoned by revenge, self-pity, resentment, or self-righteousness, do they destroy us. Jesus' wounds never became infected in this way. Jesus' spirit was never destroyed, and therefore salvation can flow from his wounds—"by his stripes we were healed" (Is 53:5). I believe that it was the profound realization of the Father's love for him that kept his wounds purified and thus life-giving. He trusted that nothing could withstand the power of his Father's love.

The passion and death of Jesus in light of the resurrection remains the most powerful proclamation of life in the face of suffering. It is a story of victory in what seemed like defeat. It is the victory of love that could not be conquered. The love between the Father and the Son could not be broken. It is the victory of forgiveness that could withstand any sin. It is the victory of compassion that remained unshaken in the face of violent injustice. It is the victory of God coming among his people in vulnerability, in woundedness, and offering the world a new vision, a new response to suffering, a response of love that destroys the power of suffering and the sting of death. This victory would speak for all time. It is the victory of inner peace.

This unique and powerful response to unjust accusations gave courage to those who followed Jesus. When the early Christians faced persecution and even death, the story of the passion was their greatest source of strength. It allowed them to find meaning in their pain, and to sustain themselves as they faced their false accusers. Mark wrote the first gospel to tell the persecuted Christians of Rome to keep their eyes on the Lord and to watch the manner in which he faced his death. They could reflect on the story of the Master and see how his silent, courageous response put the accusers on trial. They would gradually realize by the time his trial was over, that the Sanhedrin, Pilate and the crowd had clearly condemned themselves to their own deaths. Jesus remained standing in the silence of truth and was raised up on the cross as a sign of the victory of love. His witness was the source of their strength

Throughout my life, this witness of Jesus has been a profound source of inner courage and strength. When things get tough, I go to the chapel and travel the way of the cross with Jesus.

It makes me aware that even if the trials I face are unjust, my response cannot be so. I cannot stand with him in the face of his trials and then deny him by how I respond to my own trials. His quiet witness always challenges me to love again, to forgive again, to live again.

This unique response of Jesus to unjust accusations can have a powerful effect on our everyday lives. We can change the way people relate to us by the way we respond to them. Jesus' example gives us the courage to change.

One Sunday in a homily I explained the power of non-retaliation as exemplified by Jesus. A week later a young man came to me and said, "It worked, just like you said it would!" I asked him,

"What worked?" He went on to explain:

"The principle you talked about last week in church. It worked. This week one of my co-workers kept coming and nagging at me to try to get me irritated. I just went on with my work because of what you had said. Finally he asked me why I wasn't getting angry or fighting back. I just said to him, 'If I don't fight, you can't win.' That statement sent him back to his business."

The young man was excited to discover the power of non-retaliation that flows from the witness of Jesus. He shared with me the peace that he felt from that incident. Perhaps that is what the disciple of Jesus meant when he wrote, "Who, indeed, can harm you if you are committed deeply to doing what is right" (1 Pt 3:13).

As I listen to people suffering from unjust accusations by peers, relatives, or spouses, I think
about the silent witness of Jesus. His response is
very challenging, and I sometimes hesitate to sug-
gest it. If people seem open to the power of the
Master's voice, and seek to follow his word in
their lives, I challenge them not to retaliate.
However, I distinguish Jesus' genuine response of
love from merely repressing one's anger to be
poured out later on someone else. I show them
that the healthiest response to false accusations is
peaceful silence, the kind of silence we see in
Jesus. This silence asks the implicit questions,
"Why do you need to say that to me, or what is
bothering you that you need to lash out at me?"
I point out as well how such silence can help
them look within themselves and ask, "What is
wounded in me that causes me to want to fight
back?" These questions help them focus on the
real issues and address those issues with compassion and courage. I then pray with them for the
strength of Jesus to be with them to help
transform old destructive habits into life-giving
responses. People have recounted very positive
disarming results from their newly learned
responses.

The power and security of hearing the
Master's voice can change the way we live our
lives. His life example challenges us to love in a
radical way. It calls us to proclaim healing in the
face of illness, forgiveness in the face of sin, and
inner peace in the face of unjust accusations. His

passion and death tell us that it is not easy; his resurrection tells us that it is the only way. Reflecting on his unique responses in these situations and the fruits of such responses empowers us to do the same.

These and other messages of Jesus give meaning and purpose to our lives. We respond to situations with peace when we feel that his love can give meaning to every event. He assures us that there is a purpose for each of our lives. As one young woman so beautifully phrased it, "Jesus is my Savior. Because of him, my life has purpose." To have purpose in life is a great source of inner security. Knowing that there is a loving plan for us gives us courage to meet the challenges of each day in peace. As we listen to the Lord's voice day after day, we will begin to be more secure. His words will say to us in many different ways, "Do not be afraid. I am with you always." Jesus drew courage and strength from knowing that his Father was journeying with him in life. The words of Jesus assure us of the same divine companionship. The Master's voice tells us that we never walk alone.

PRAYER FOR INNER PEACE

Lord, the example of your life tells me of an inner peace that I truly desire. Your care for people who were ill or living in sin shows that you are always with me, helping me find healing and peace. I thank you for your response of compassion toward all who needed you, for I know that I need you often. Give me the peace of knowing that you are with me as I try to proclaim the message of your love. Help me to feel you at my side in trials, that my responses to injustice will tell others of the power of your love. Lord, I am grateful that you never abandon me, even when I think that you have. Help me not to abandon you, but to keep my ears attuned to your voice, the voice that gives me peace. Amen.

GOD'S WORDS OF PEACE FOR REFLECTION

Keep me, O God, for in you I take refuge;
    I say to the LORD, "My Lord are you.
    Apart from you I have no good." . . .
O LORD, my allotted portion and my cup,
    you it is who hold fast my lot. . . .
I set the LORD ever before me;
    with him at my right hand I shall not be
        disturbed. . . .
You will show me the path to life,
    fullness of joys in your presence,
    the delights at your right hand forever.
                            (Psalm 16:1-2,5,8,11)

"How blest are the poor in spirit: the reign
    of God is theirs.
Blest too are the sorrowing; they shall be
    consoled.
Blest are the lowly; they shall inherit the
    land.
Blest are they who hunger and thirst for
    holiness; they shall have their fill.
Blest are they who show mercy; mercy shall
    be theirs.
Blest are the single-hearted for they shall see
    God.
Blest too the peacemakers; they shall be
    called sons of God.
Blest are those persecuted for holiness sake;
    the reign of God is theirs.
Blest are you when they insult you and
    persecute you and utter every kind of
    slander against you because of me.

Be glad and rejoice, for your reward is great
    in heaven;
they persecuted the prophets before you in
    the very same way."

(Matthew 5:3-12)

Jesus said, "I am the good shepherd.
I know my sheep
and my sheep know me
in the same way that the Father knows me
and I know the Father;
for these sheep I will give my life."

(John 10:14-15)

We know that God makes all things work together
for the good of those who have been called accord-
ing to his decree. . . . If God is for us, who can be
against us? . . . Who will separate us from the love
of Christ? . . . For I am certain that neither death
nor life, neither angels nor principalities, neither
the present nor the future, nor powers, neither
height nor depth nor any other creature, will be
able to separate us from the love of God that comes
to us in Christ Jesus, our Lord.

(Romans 8:28,31,35,38-39)

Other appropriate readings:

Psalm 31:2-4	Luke 18:27
Psalm 121	Luke 22:19-20
Isaiah 42:1-4	John 1:11-12
Isaiah 53:5, 7, 11	John 3:14-17
Ezekiel 34:11-12, 15-16	Revelations 22:17
Matthew 28:20	

CHAPTER 5

Peter and John answered, "Judge for yourselves whether it is right in God's sight for us to obey you rather than God. Surely we cannot help speaking of what we have heard and seen."

(Acts 4:19-20)

ONE WHO FOUND COURAGE AND PEACE

If the example of any life in the scriptures gives us a realistic picture of the struggle from fear to courage, and the power of the Master's voice on that journey, it is the story of Peter. He could have gone in many directions, but in his own fearful and stumbling way, he kept journeying with the Lord—a road that led ultimately to inner peace. His journey is very human. He is one of us. We can let his life speak to us. His example shows us a way to arrive at lasting peace.

Peter was not always courageous. He displayed a certain zeal at times for new things, but his courage usually failed him just when he needed it most. He was ready to let go of the nets and travel to unknown territory (Mk 1:16-18). He offered his home as a place of rest for this traveling preacher, a gesture that may have taken more courage than we first imagine

(Mk 1:29). He seemed to speak up first among the apostles, yet at times it would appear that he had spoken too soon (Mk 8:31-33). We might travel with Peter for a bit to see what kept him on the road.

Peter's initial desire to step out and experience new things was the quality that probably got him into the most trouble, but it also led to the most growth. Recall the time the disciples were in the boat being tossed by the storm, and Jesus came walking toward them on the water (Mt 14:24-33). All of the disciples were scared. Peter was as afraid as any of them, but even in his fear he was ready to step out on the water. He dared to step beyond his fear at the invitation of Jesus. His daring spirit propelled him out of the boat and onto the water. The story tells us that "when he perceived how strong the wind was," he became frightened and began to sink. Once again, however, in his fear he called upon the Lord. He did not reach back for his old security, but kept grasping for the one who would give him real courage. His readiness to plunge in, even if it meant getting wet, was the quality that kept his journey to greater courage alive.

We get the impression from the gospel that Peter watched Jesus closely. He always seemed to be the first to answer when any question was asked (Mk 8:29-30; Lk 8:45), or to ask for an explanation of Jesus' actions when they were not clear to him (Mk 11:21; Mt 15:15). He must have been proud to be with the one who cured the lepers, the paralyzed, and the blind. He had to have been amazed as Jesus stood in courage before the Pharisees and scribes who plotted against him. He watched Jesus handle the questions about forgiveness at Capernaum (Mk 2:1-12), the Sabbath dispute in the synagogue (Mk 3:1-6), and the false accusations about the source of his power over evil spirits (Mk 3:22-30). Peter watched a person who knew what he was about, who offered a healing response to the sick, a forgiving response to sinners, and a courageous response to accusers. He was learning how to go beyond fear. He was seeing how inner peace could set people free.

He still must have been afraid when Jesus sent him on the first mission (Mk 6:7-13). Perhaps the fact that he could go with a fellow disciple was some consolation. I'm sure that if he could have taken his fishing net, he would have been more secure. Some things are just nice to have close to us when we are in new territory! Whether it was courage or just the excitement of being on the road, we get the impression that all the disciples passed this initial test.

When Jesus started mentioning Jerusalem and impending death (Mk 8:31-33), Peter's fears again came to the fore. We can all imagine how we would have felt. The journey toward inner peace is not easy, but the gentle understanding of Jesus makes it possible. Traveling with the Master had been getting comfortable for Peter, or at least feasible, but the mention of possible death brought a quick alternative plan from the disciples' spokesman. Jesus simply invites Peter to get back into his following because he is about to teach him his most powerful message concerning courage and peace. He would take the disciples through their greatest fear—fear of death. He would reveal to them the paradox of life; namely, if you are not afraid of losing your life, no one can take it from you.

From that moment on, Peter was to see a new dimension in the Master's life. I'm sure he felt a deeper seriousness in the Master's voice, and a greater strength in his actions. He probably needed to see that glimpse of the resurrection on the mountain of Transfiguration (Mk 9:2-8) to keep up his courage on his journey to Jerusalem. Peter probably listened with more intensity to the words of Jesus and reflected on the fact that Jesus continued to pour out his life little by little in generous service to those who sought life.

He had to be amazed as Jesus found meaning in his impending suffering by identifying himself with the Servant of the Lord described by the prophet Isaiah (Is 52:13 to 53:12). Even though Peter did not understand what he first heard, his ears gradually became attentive to the meaning of the Master's message. Between the lines Peter could hear that Jesus was making some powerful decisions, and the words of the prophet were giving meaning to his journey. Phrases from his pas-

sion predictions had the ring of prophetic ut-
terances. Jesus was saying that he "would suffer
much . . . be delivered over . . . for the salvation
of many" (Mk 8:31; 9:31; 10:45), and the words
began to make sense. The Master could make his
journey to Jerusalem with the words of the
prophet Isaiah giving meaning to his actions.
"Through his suffering my Servant shall justify
many and their guilt he shall bear" (Is 53:11).
Jesus was not running away; he was not angry at
anyone; he was simply preparing to face death
with courage in order to bring life to his people.
This way of finding meaning in his suffering was
unique, and Peter must have watched the process
very closely. As a disciple he knew that he would
have to do the same. Like Peter, we can learn
much from the example of the Master in this
regard.

Peter, it seems, gained great courage from the
words of Jesus, yet when reality hit, old fears
showed themselves with uncontrollable force. At
the last supper Peter was proud of his courage.
He assured the Master, "Even though all are
shaken in faith, it will not be that way with me.
. . . Even if I have to die with you, I will not
deny you" (Mk 14:29,31). He felt ready for the
new challenge. The Master knew that courage
did not grow so quickly, *but it would grow.*

The sharp edges of the guards' swords and
the voice of an unruly crowd wore Peter's
courage thin, and with the rest of the disciples he
left the Master standing alone. He is overcome

with fear again, but he has not lost his daring spirit. He continues to travel with the Lord, even if at a distance. This trait would allow him to learn firsthand the power of truthful silence. Perhaps this part of Peter's journey resonates within us. We wish to follow Jesus but sometimes it seems safer to stay at a distance. Peter's life encourages us to keep following the Master even if we do not feel close to him, for he wants us to learn real peace.

Even from a distance, Peter could see and hear the false accusations leveled against his Lord. Despite his fear, he watched the God-man battered by ruthless interrogations and threats of death, and the God-man simply stood in silent courage (Mk 14:61). The one who had always spoken the truth, and who was moved with compassion for anyone who was hurting, now stood silently in the face of false accusations and harsh treatment and demonstrated the power of his words. The memory of Jesus' example must have been deeply ingrained in Peter's mind and heart. That evening he learned the power of inner courage, and even though that same night he would back away in fear denying the Master, there *would* come a day when his victory over fear would be won.

Peter's inability to stand in courage with the Master tells us that he was human; his sorrow over that inability tells us that he would try again. His persevering heart, together with the realization that courage comes from the Lord, set him back on his journey toward inner security and peace. His ability to humbly admit failure and begin again speaks to me as I seek to walk in the footsteps of the Master. Perhaps it speaks to all of us.

In the absence of the Lord, fear abounded among all the disciples. As his Spirit began to unify their hearts and reveal his living presence in their midst, fear gave way to courage, and discord gave way to peace. Peter could recall the words that the Master had said at sea, "Get hold of yourselves! It is I. Do not be afraid!" (Mt 14:27). He was again ready to step out beyond the closed doors. The crowds became less of a threat as he saw the words of Jesus bring one person after another to repentant faith. His courage grew as he watched the name of Jesus strengthen the limbs of a crippled man (Acts 3:1-10). His journey toward courage and inner peace was reaching its end. He could feel the Master with him, and nothing would keep him from following the message of that voice.

The final test of Peter's courage came as he faced the leaders of the land. Through the power of Jesus' love he had healed a crippled man and proclaimed the promise of the resurrection, and now he was on trial. The Acts of the Apostles indicates to us that by this time Peter had learned the secret of inner security (Acts 4:5-22; 5:17-42). In the power of the Holy Spirit he simply proclaimed the truth about his Lord and then stood silently in the power of that truth.

His self-assurance, together with that of John, left
the Sanhedrin in fear and amazement. Peter had
discovered the power of peace in the Lord, and
no one was going to stop him from proclaiming
it.

Like Jesus, Peter did not become defensive in
response to accusations, for he had learned that
the truth defends itself. He did not become fearful in the face of threats, for he knew that the
Sanhedrin was only displaying its own fears. He
knew what he was about. He knew who he
believed in, and in peaceful courage he watched
the leaders of the land condemn themselves to
the prison of disbelief and fear. He accepted the
pain of the scourging "with joy" for he knew that
his victory over fear was bearing its fruit. His victory was instilling courage in those who watched
him. The message of his Master was being proclaimed in his witness. The community of
disciples learned from him and from each other.
Each of their steps in courage, each of their vic-
tories over fear, made the community a more
powerful witness of the peace that only Jesus can
give.

Peter's life example leaves us hopeful as we
struggle with various forms of fear in our lives.
His life shows us the importance of keeping our
eyes on the Master. It demonstrates the fruits of
always reaching for the Master's hand, even in
the midst of our fears and failures. His life por-
trays the deep security of knowing that the Lord
will never abandon us even when we abandon

him. Peter shows us a very human journey that found its end in the author of life himself. Jesus saw courage in Peter before Peter saw courage in himself. He sees the same in us. As long as Peter stayed with the journey and persisted in stepping beyond fear, the Master knew that he would win the victory of inner security and peaceful courage. That victory is ours for the same price, and the Master keeps telling us that it is possible.

PRAYER FOR PERSEVERANCE

Lord, I thank you for the patience that you had with Peter as he grew in courage and peace. It tells me that you will be patient with me on my journey toward inner peace and security. His life shows me the power of your love and the depth of your understanding. Help me to feel you walking at my side as I seek to let go of old fears. Give me the insight to understand your purpose for my life and the zeal to fulfill that purpose. Teach me to persevere on my journey with you, even if I fail at times. Thank you for telling me through the life of Peter that you will always be with me. Your love for him tells me that I am lovable, and that anything is possible. Thank you for calling me to be your disciple and letting me know how much you love me. Thank you, Lord. Amen.

GOD'S WORDS OF PEACE FOR REFLECTION

> To you I lift up my soul,
>   O LORD, my God.
> In you I trust; let me not be put to shame,
>   let not my enemies exult over me.
> No one who waits for you shall be put
>   to shame;
>   those shall be put to shame who heedlessly
>   break faith.
> Your ways, O LORD, make known to me;
>   teach me your paths,
> Guide me in your truth and teach me,
>   for you are God my savior,
>   and for you I wait all the day.
>
> (Psalm 25:1-5)

> God indeed is my savior;
>   I am confident and unafraid.
> My strength and my courage is the LORD,
>   and he has been my savior.
> With joy you will draw water
>   at the fountain of salvation, and say on
>   that day;
> Give thanks to the LORD; acclaim his
>   name.
>
> (Isaiah 12:2-4)

Jesus then said to the Twelve, "Do you want to leave me too?" Simon Peter answered him, "Lord, to whom shall we go? You have the words of eternal life. We have come to believe; we are convinced that you are God's holy one."

(John 6:67-69)

Then Peter, filled with the Holy Spirit, spoke up: "Leaders of the people! Elders! If we must answer today for a good deed done to a cripple and explain how he was restored to health, then you and all the people of Israel must realize that it was done in the name of Jesus Christ the Nazorean whom you crucified and whom God raised from the dead. In the power of that name this man stands before you perfectly sound. . . . Observing the self-assurance of Peter and John, and realizing that the speakers were uneducated men of no standing, the questioners were amazed.

(Acts 4:8-10,13)

Other appropriate readings:

Psalm 3:1-7	Luke 24:36-39
Psalm 27:1-2	John 12:24-25
Psalm 138:1, 3, 7-8	Philippians 4:13
Jeremiah 15:19-20	1 Peter 2:9-10
Luke 12:4	1 Peter 3:13-15

CHAPTER **6**

Jesus said, " 'Peace' is my farewell to you, my peace is my gift to you; I do not give it to you as the world gives peace."

(John 14:27)

A VISION OF
LASTING PEACE

The journey toward inner security in God is the only journey that brings lasting peace. It is Jesus' vision of peace. As we have seen, he addressed the real issues deep inside the people he met, and offered them his gift. His dealings with people were very personal and individual. With gentle care he set people free, free to be at peace. His words and his actions brought lasting peace to all who chose to disarm themselves and accept his *gift*. His love calmed their fears and gave them the security to let go of old defenses and to begin to live freely. I truly believe in this vision of peace. I believe that his gift is being offered to every person, for he came that we might know true peace.

As indicated earlier, it is important to distinguish clearly Jesus' silent inner peace from mere repression of feelings. Jesus' silent witness was not an admission of defeat or a retreat into self-pity, but a powerful proclamation that he knew the Father's voice and felt the Father's love. Because of that love, he could proclaim truth and justice with a peacefulness that never retaliated or became defensive. He does not tell us to deny our feelings, but to let *his feelings for us* be our strength and our peace. He does not teach us to accept falsehood or injustice without a response; he, rather, teaches us a response that is born of peace with ourselves and with our God. He does not teach us to act helplessly, but to listen to the real helper, so that our responses to people and situations flow from his love in us. His vision of peace is not a denial of who we are, but a proclamation of *who he is for us*. His vision of true peace calls us to proclaim the truth of his message and then silently let our life witness to that message.

This movement toward true peace begins when we realize that things can be different, that there are alternative responses to life situations. It begins with the awareness that the love of Jesus can make all things new. We do not need to stay locked in old patterns or imprisoned in old feelings. We can find forgiveness and healing in Jesus. We can begin to make different responses to situations when we realize that Jesus is with us.

When we begin reacting differently to events or to people, we cause others around us to respond differently also. This process may at first disrupt a quasi-peace that seems somewhat comfortable, but if it is done with the guidance of the Master's voice, it will lead to lasting peace. I believe that this is what Jesus meant when he said that there may be divisions for a time before arriving at a deeper lasting peace (Lk 12:49-53). He makes us aware that some disruption may occur even within families before true peace is accomplished. I have noticed this to be true in a number of cases.

When I work with certain people in spiritual direction and growth, they mention at times that their spouses or children are bothered by their growth. I ask them to closely examine their words and attitudes to see if they are being judgmental in any way. If not, I encourage them to quietly continue in the process that is helping them grow closer to the Lord. Their new peace, their new patience, will call others to examine their own spirituality. Their new responses may wrestle others loose from comfortable patterns and in that sense cause divisions, but I assure them that their quiet, humble journey can only lead to greater ultimate peace.

At times I find that people who are shaken loose by another person's peacefulness are really searching for that peacefulness themselves. They sometimes need just such a quiet "invitation" to make their own first step toward peace. Sometimes their initial hostile reaction is really part of their final defense. Our quiet peace and gentle patience can help them dismantle those final weapons.

Sometimes we may find ourselves in a pattern of doing battle and we may wonder where the Lord's vision of peace fits in. An example of this situation is the woman who came to me because she and her husband could not talk without getting into an argument. As we talked she described how they would get angry at each other over such little things and immediately an argument would follow. I asked her what would happen if she did not fight back. I asked her if she knew why she needed to return comments when he made "false accusations." Gradually she realized that he was tearing loose memories from her past that were very painful. I convinced her to spend her time letting the Lord minister his healing love upon her painful memories.

"But he's going to be more angry if I don't respond," she said.

"Yes," I said, "probably for a time he will, but if you remain peaceful as the Lord heals your past wounds, your peace will force him to look at himself. Then he will have to deal with the question of why he needs to lash out at you. Changing your response will make him look within himself and deal with the real issues. If he doesn't, the burden will be on him, and you will be at peace." This woman came to understand that changing her inner responses through inner healing prayer may take time, but I assured her that it was the only way I knew to arrive at any kind of lasting peace. I encouraged her to find a praying community in which she could be continually soaked in the Lord's word and his love. I told her that one of the most helpful responses she could make to her situation was to invite him daily into her past life and let his caring presence minister to her areas of pain.

Changing our responses takes time and effort. It means making the journey toward inner security and peace. As we have seen in the earlier chapters of this book, it may involve the admission of sin and repentance, followed by an experience of forgiveness. It may involve a prayerful walk into past memories that still have a hold upon us and cause us to make unhealthy and even harmful responses. It will involve developing a process of quieting ourselves and listening to the voice of the Master. All of this takes time and probably the help of some caring person or community that will guide us and remain with us on this journey, but the journey to inner peace is truly worth it. It is the only way to live, at least as Jesus defines life. It is the life he came to bring.

This journey is worth it not only for ourselves, but for all those we know. It is the most precious gift we can offer to those we love, and the way we offer it to them is by living it as fully as we can. The journey of Peter shows us that as we overcome our fears and insecurities with the peace of Jesus, we can then give the gift to others who see us and listen to us.

Living with the inner peace found in Jesus proclaims the central message of the gospel louder than any words. When our relationship with the Peacemaker gives our lives a confident purpose and direction, people will notice. The way we respond to situations, especially difficult ones, will demonstrate to them the power of true peace. That is why the life witness of Jesus was so powerful to all who met him. He lived in peace.

Another example of the power of a peaceful inner life is the story of Paul's imprisonment in Philippi (Acts 16:16-34). Paul delivered a slave girl from an evil spirit and ended up getting flogged and thrown into prison for it. He could have gotten angry and bitter for this injustice done to him. He would have been justified in being upset, but instead he sits in prison "praying and singing hymns to God." This unique response of inner security and peace caused the prisoners to notice, and ultimately brought the jailer and his whole family to new life in the Lord.

This response of inner peace in unjust situations continues to change people's lives. I discovered an example of this as I talked with some of our college students last summer. I could hear how well they had learned this peaceful response. They had truly interiorized the message of Jesus. Six of them had sat in an abortion clinic in order to rescue unborn children from death. In this attempt, they were arrested for trespassing. They never resisted but continued to proclaim the sacredness of human life. At their trial they defended themselves knowing that their Defender was with them. Like Paul, they had

learned from Jesus how to handle unjust accusations. They peacefully showed that they were trying to help save lives. They knew that if they
had broken into a car to save the life of a suf-
focating dog, they would have been legally
acquitted. They had come into an abortion clinic
to save the lives of unborn babies and, in this
case, they were found legally guilty of trespassing.
With the Lord's help they remained peaceful and
kind to their accusers. As a sign of love, they
gave a rose to the lawyer who argued against
them. Their peaceful acceptance of their sentence
had a profound effect on the jury for, after the
trial, some of its members came and encouraged
them to keep up their efforts on behalf of human
life. They knew that the peace of Jesus, which
they felt inside, had "won" their case.

The central part of Jesus' vision of peace is
his message about the resurrection from the dead.
The security of the belief in the resurrection from
the dead allows people to face situations in a new
way. With the coming of Jesus and the change in
those who followed him, the world had to deal
with a new phenomenon, namely, what to do
with people who believed in eternal life. The inner security of knowing that life goes on makes a
big difference in how people face death, or the
threat of death. Perhaps that is why the manner
of Jesus' death had such a profound transforming
effect on the centurion who watched the event.
Observing the way Jesus faced death, the Roman
centurion declared, "Clearly this man was the
Son of God!" (Mk 15:39).

As the early Christians faced death with
courage, people who observed them were at-
tracted to the source of their courage. Still today
the witnesses of Christian martyrs speak of true
peace. Every human being longs for inner peace,
and when they see it in another, they search for
its origin. Those who try to put an end to the
people who believe in the resurrection gradually
learn that they cannot kill people with an eternal
vision in their heart. Their courage in the face of
death only attracts more people to the Lord and
his gift of lasting peace. Perhaps each of us knows
people who exude this inner peace and strength.
Their witness draws us to want the same. Even
though they may not have to face physical death,
the way they die to themselves and accept difficult situations tells us that they live with real
peace. This security in Jesus' peace helps them
face life and live it to the full. The reason Jesus
came into the world was to give us this fullness
of life (Jn 10:10).

The realization that the Lord walks alongside
us through life, and even carries us at times, is
truly a powerful gift. Maybe that is why the
poem *Footprints in the Sand* is so inspiring and
uplifting to so many people. Perhaps that is why
Psalm 23 is so comforting when we have just experienced the loss of a loved one. We draw peace
from knowing that we do not walk alone. Jesus'
vision of peace is based on the promise that he is
with us always.

I believe that the most profound and unique

message that Jesus gave to the world was the witness of his inner peace. He talked with anyone; he touched anyone; he ate with anyone, and no one could stop him. He courageously went about giving people life and making them face the real issues of growth within themselves. When people resisted, he never retaliated, but continued on the path that his Father laid out for him. He made it clear that the peace he promised began in the heart of each person. His accepting love gave everyone the space they needed to discover that peace, if they chose to do so. He never forced anyone. His quiet peace simply offered a new vision of peace to all who met him.

Jesus' vision of peace that begins in the hearts of individuals gave new meaning to the vision of peace depicted in the book of the prophet Isaiah (Is 2:1-5). The imagery in Isaiah speaks of a universal vision of peace when all nations will gather and listen to God's plan for peace. It gives a picture of nations bending their one-time weapons into tools for producing food. Jesus' message tells us that the way this will come about is with one person at a time. The peace he promises pervades the world through one heart after another. His knowledge that final peace will come allows him to be patient and gentle with each one of his people. Even if we get frustrated with the time it takes to find inner peace, or begin thinking that it will never happen to us, he continues to believe in us. He never gets discouraged because his vision of peace is far beyond our understanding. He sees new life in places where we would not dream that life was even possible. His vision of peace gives us hope, it gives us courage as it gave Peter courage to believe that nothing is impossible with God.

As we listen to reports about fighting and wars around the world, it is hard to envision peace. We could get discouraged and even frightened at the possibilities of massive world destruction. Jesus tells us that we will only get frightened if the fear is within ourselves. His vision for world peace does not begin with national power, but with the power of courageous inner peace. The security he offered to his followers was not the security of weapons, but the inner security of knowing that they were loved and would be loved eternally. He offers that same security to you and me.

I cannot envision peace beginning with nations, but I can envision peace beginning with one person after another, the peace that comes from knowing the Creator and his purpose for our lives. As I go about my ministry, I do see one person and then another discovering the freeing power of the Lord's mercy. I do see people dropping their defenses and experiencing the healing power of divine Love. I do hear one person after another disarming their language of cutting words and jabbing remarks as they bathe themselves in the mystery of the silent Witness. The vision of Isaiah is becoming a reality as inner peace grows in one person after another. I can envision inner peace pervading the world, a peace that flows from individuals quieting themselves and listening to the Master's voice. I can envision a peace that flows from a journey inward, a peace that the world cannot give, a peace that the world may not fully understand. It is the peace of inner security that does not need weapons. It is the peace of submission to the God-man who "submitted, and opened not his mouth" (Is 53:7).

Jesus left us his peace as his farewell gift (Jn 14:27). Inner peace is *the* gift of Jesus. That gift is promised to you and to me. It is our security. No fear can withstand the persistent love with which it is offered to us. My hope is that this little book will help you understand and experience that gift, and the love with which it is given to us. My hope is that together we will discover in an ever deeper way the preciousness and the power of that gift. My dream is that this gift, this peace, will pervade the whole world, for if life is worth living, it is worth living in peace.

PRAYER FOR THE VISION
OF TRUE PEACE

Lord, your vision of peace is broad and powerful and yet it is gentle and personal. I long to live in that peace. Fill my heart, my mind, my whole being with your gift of lasting peace. Calm all my inner fears with your mercy and healing love. Help me to quiet myself each day, that I may soak in the peace of your words. Let me feel you always at my side as I face the challenges of each day. Teach me to be courageous and gentle in proclaiming the message of your love. I thank you, Lord, for I know that you will stay by my side as I surrender more and more of my life into your hands. I thank you for seeing so much good in me. I thank you that you have never forgotten me or left me alone. Thank you for giving yourself so totally that I might know real peace. You truly are a faithful Lover. Thank you. Amen.

GOD'S WORDS OF PEACE FOR REFLECTION

Only in God is my soul at rest;
 from him comes my salvation.
He only is my rock and my salvation,
 my stronghold; I shall not be disturbed at
  all.

           (Psalm 62:2-3)

On the evening of that first day of the week, even though the disciples had locked the doors of the place where they were for fear of the Jews, Jesus came and stood before them. "Peace be with you," he said. When he said this, he showed them his hands and his side. At the sight of the Lord the disciples rejoiced. "Peace be with you," he said again. "As the Father has sent me, so I send you."

           (John 20:19-21)

Therefore I am content with weakness, with mistreatment, with distress, with persecution and difficulties for the sake of Christ; for when I am powerless, it is then that I am strong.

         (2 Corinthians 12:10)

Then I saw new heavens and a new earth. The former heavens and the former earth had passed away, and the sea was no longer. I also saw a new Jerusalem, the holy city, coming down out of heaven from God, beautiful as a bride prepared to meet her husband. I heard a loud voice from the throne cry out: "This is God's dwelling among men. He shall dwell with them and they shall be his people and he shall be their God who is always with them. He shall wipe every tear from their eyes, and there shall be no more death or mourning, crying out or pain, for the former world has passed away." The One who sat on the throne said to me, "See, I make all things new!"

(Revelations 21:1-5)

Other appropriate readings:

Psalm 23:1-4	John 10:10
Isaiah 2:2-4	John 11:25-26
Jeremiah 1:4-8	John 14:27
Zephaniah 3:14-15	Romans 8:11
Mark 10:45	2 Corinthians 5:1
John 8:31-32	Philippians 3:13-14, 16

HELPFUL READING

Baars, M.D., Conrad. *Born Only Once.* Chicago: Franciscan Herald Press. 1975. (Speaks of the healing power of God's affirming love, and the power we have within us to love and affirm each other.)

Bodo, O.F.M., Murray. *The Journey and the Dream.* Cincinnati: St. Anthony Messenger Press. 1972. (A beautiful and poetic story of the journey of St. Francis of Assisi as he followed his Lord.)

Dobson, Theodore. *How to Pray For Spiritual Growth.* Ramsey, NJ: Paulist Press. 1982. (A comprehensive and prayerful description of how we can grow closer to the Lord through inner healing.)

Feider, Paul. *The Christian Search for Meaning in Suffering.* Mystic, CT: Twenty-Third Publications. 1980. (A view of how Jesus wishes to heal sickness and yet finds meaning in his own suffering.)

Green, S.J., Thomas. *When the Well Runs Dry.* Notre Dame, IN: Ave Maria Press. 1979. (Some very helpful ideas concerning what to do when we do not seem to be able to pray.)

Hakenewerth, S.M., Quentin. *In His Likeness.* St. Louis: Maryhurst Press. 1977. (Gives clear ways of quieting ourselves that the Lord may purify our lives and draw us closer to himself.)

Linn, S.J., Matthew and Dennis. *Healing of Memories.* Ramsey, NJ: Paulist Press. 1974. (Guides us through the steps of letting the love of God heal our past memories especially through forgiveness.)

Linn, S.J., Matthew and Dennis. *Healing Life's Hurts.* Ramsey, NJ: Paulist Press. 1978. (An in-depth study and explanation of the process of healing through prayer and human caring.)

McNeill, Donald; Morrison, Douglas; and Nouwen, Henri. *Compassion.* Garden City, NY: Doubleday and Company. 1982. (A reflective book on the power of God's compassion and our own compassion.)

Scanlan, Michael. *Inner Healing.* Ramsey, NJ: Paulist Press. 1974. (Focuses on the peace of Jesus and his desire to heal our inner being.)

Shlemon, Barbara. *Healing Prayer.* Notre Dame, IN: Ave Maria Press. 1972. (Takes us simply through the process of healing prayer, showing us the steps to wholeness.)

Shlemon, Barbara. *Healing the Hidden Self.* Notre Dame, IN: Ave Maria Press. 1982. (Describes areas within ourselves that may not be at peace, and then gives some beautiful examples and prayers to help us find healing.)